The Confidence Rx

Overcome Self-Doubt and Improve Self-Esteem and Image

Olufemi Olaseni, MDiv

from various sources. Please consult a licensed professional before attempting any techniques outlined in this book.

By reading this document, the reader agrees that under no circumstances is the author responsible for any losses, direct or indirect, that are incurred as a result of the use of the information contained within this document, including, but not limited to, errors, omissions, or inaccuracies.

Table of Contents

Introduction

Confidence is a quality that has the power to transform lives, shaping individuals into their best selves and propelling them toward success. In the realm of personal growth, confidence stands as a beacon of strength and self-assurance, capable of unlocking doors to opportunities and heights previously thought unattainable. This book explores the intricate tapestry of confidence, dissecting its essence, exploring the ramifications of self-doubt, and providing a road map for individuals seeking transformation.

The Power of Confidence

Confidence, at its core, is the unwavering belief in oneself and abilities. It serves as a catalyst for personal development, enabling individuals to navigate challenges with resilience and determination. The power of confidence lies in its ability to shape thoughts, emotions, and actions in alignment with one's aspirations. When harnessed effectively, confidence acts as a shield against doubts and insecurities, paving the way for achievement and fulfillment.

Defining Confidence and Its Impact on Personal Growth

To truly understand the impact of confidence on personal growth, one must first grasp the essence of this elusive quality. Confidence is not merely a superficial display of bravado but an inner reservoir of self-belief and conviction. It fuels ambition, drives innovation, and emboldens individuals to pursue their dreams with unwavering determination.

In the journey of personal growth, confidence acts as a pillar of support, providing the necessary foundation for individuals to strive toward their full potential. It instills courage in the face of adversity, fosters resilience in times of uncertainty, and empowers individuals to overcome obstacles with grace and tenacity. Without confidence, personal growth stagnates, as doubts and insecurities hinder progress and breed complacency.

The Role of Self-Doubt and Its Consequences

Conversely, self-doubt stands as the antithesis of confidence, casting shadows of uncertainty and fear over one's ambitions and aspirations. Rooted in insecurities and past failures, self-doubt erodes confidence, sowing seeds of hesitation and indecision.

It is a silent saboteur, stealthily undermining one's self-esteem and potential, leading to missed opportunities and unfulfilled dreams.

The consequences of self-doubt are far-reaching. They permeate every aspect of one's life and stifle growth and progress. Self-doubt fosters a mindset of limitation and defeat, constraining individuals within the confines of their fears and insecurities. Over time, self-doubt becomes a self-fulfilling prophecy, shaping realities based on perceived inadequacies rather than actual capabilities.

Setting the Stage for Transformation

Amidst the tumultuous interplay of confidence and self-doubt lies the opportunity for transformation. The stage is set for individuals to embark on a journey of self-discovery, shedding old patterns of thinking and behavior in favor of boldness and self-assurance. This book serves as a guiding light, illuminating the path toward personal growth and empowerment.

In the pursuit of transformation, it is essential to cultivate a mindset of possibility and resilience, drawing inspiration from timeless wisdom and spiritual truths:

I can do all things through Christ who strengthens me. – Philippians 4:13

But those who wait on the Lord shall renew their strength; they shall mount up with wings like eagles, they shall run and not be weary, they shall walk and not faint. —Isaiah 40:31

These scriptural passages remind us of the inherent strength and potential that lies within each individual. By aligning our beliefs with a higher purpose and divine providence, we can transcend self-doubt and embrace the boundless possibilities of a confident and purpose-driven life. These words set the stage for a deep exploration of confidence, self-doubt, and transformation, weaving together insightful perspectives and spiritual wisdom to inspire and empower readers on their journey toward personal growth and success.

Not that we are sufficient of ourselves to think of anything as being from ourselves, but our sufficiency is from God. –2 Corinthians 3:5

Chapter 1:

Understanding Self-Doubt:

Unmasking the Inner Critic

In the journey of self-discovery and personal growth, understanding self-doubt plays a crucial role in unmasking the inner critic that often undermines our confidence and limits our potential. This chapter looks into the complex nature of self-doubt, exploring the common patterns that manifest in our thoughts and behaviors. By shedding light on these patterns, we can recognize and address the inner critic that holds us back from realizing our true worth and capabilities.

Identifying Common Self-Doubt Patterns

Self-doubt is a pervasive issue that affects individuals from all walks of life, regardless of age, gender, or background (Pinto, 2023). It can manifest in various ways, often presenting as negative self-talk, fear of failure, imposter syndrome, and perfectionism.

Recognizing these common patterns is the first step toward overcoming self-doubt and reclaiming self-confidence.

Negative self-talk is perhaps one of the most prevalent self-doubt patterns, where our inner critic constantly feeds us with thoughts of inadequacy, unworthiness, and self-criticism. This toxic dialogue erodes our self-esteem and creates a barrier to personal growth and success. The scriptural passage from 2 Corinthians 3:5 resonates with this pattern, reminding us that our sufficiency does not come from ourselves but from God. By acknowledging our limitations and seeking support from a source beyond ourselves, we can transcend self-doubt and tap into our inherent strengths.

Fear of failure is another common self-doubt pattern that keeps individuals from pursuing their goals and aspirations. The inner critic amplifies our doubts and insecurities, convincing us that we are not capable of success. However, the truth is that failure is an inevitable part of the learning process, and each setback brings us closer to our goals if we choose to persevere. Embracing a growth mindset, as advocated in the scripture, can help us reframe our perception of failure as an opportunity for growth and self-improvement.

Perfectionism is yet another self-doubt pattern that drives individuals to set unrealistically high standards for themselves, leading to chronic dissatisfaction and self-criticism. The inner critic constantly whispers that we are not good enough unless we achieve perfection in every aspect of our lives, sabotaging our efforts and perpetuating feelings of inadequacy. However, true growth and fulfillment come from embracing our imperfections and learning to appreciate the journey rather than fixating on the destination.

Exploring the Origins of Negative Self-Talk

Negative self-talk is a pervasive self-doubt pattern that can have a profound impact on our mental health and well-being. Negative self-talk refers to the critical or unhelpful thoughts and beliefs we have about ourselves, often based on past experiences or insecurities. The origins of negative self-talk are complex and varied and can be influenced by a range of factors, such as childhood experiences, societal pressures, and personal expectations.

Childhood experiences are often significant in shaping our belief systems and self-talk patterns. Negative self-talk may have its roots in early childhood experiences, such as parental criticism, neglect, or abuse, which can lead to feelings of unworthiness and internalized shame. Children who grow up in environments where their accomplishments and self-esteem are constantly undermined may develop negative self-talk patterns that persist into adulthood. For example, a child who is consistently told they are not good enough or that their efforts are not valued may grow up with a pervasive sense of self-doubt and a harsh inner critic.

Societal pressures and expectations can also contribute to negative self-talk patterns. In a culture, especially in the Western world, that prioritizes achievement, success, and appearance, individuals may internalize the message that they must meet certain standards to be considered worthy or valuable. This can contribute to feelings of inadequacy and self-criticism as individuals compare themselves to others and strive for unattainable ideals. For example, a person who constantly compares themselves to their peers and views themselves as inferior may develop a negative self-talk pattern that reinforces this belief.

Personal expectations and beliefs can also shape our self-talk patterns. When we hold unrealistic expectations of ourselves, such as perfectionism, we can set ourselves up for feelings of failure and disappointment. When we do not meet these unrealistic expectations, our inner critic may amplify our self-doubt with negative self-talk. Personal beliefs such as a fixed mindset (believing that our abilities are predetermined and unchangeable) can also lead to negative self-talk patterns that reinforce limiting beliefs and hinder personal growth.

Identifying the origins of negative self-talk is crucial for developing strategies to manage and overcome it. One effective approach is cognitive behavioral therapy (CBT), which aims to identify and challenge negative thought patterns and beliefs through cognitive restructuring and behavioral interventions. By examining the origins of negative self-talk and associated beliefs, individuals can develop a more compassionate and empowering relationship with themselves. Engaging in positive self-talk, mindfulness practices, biblical meditation, and self-care can also help mitigate the impact of negative self-talk and cultivate a more positive self-image.

Strategies to Recognize and Challenge Self-Doubt

Recognizing and challenging self-doubt is crucial to personal growth and mental well-being. By identifying the patterns of self-doubt and actively working to challenge them, individuals can develop a more confident and resilient mindset. Here are a few practical strategies to recognize and challenge self-doubt:

- **Utilize Mindfulness and Self-Awareness:** Practicing mindfulness can help individuals become more attuned to their thoughts and emotions, allowing them to recognize the presence of self-doubt. By cultivating self-awareness, individuals can identify the specific triggers and thought patterns associated with self-doubt, enabling them to intervene and challenge negative self-talk as it arises.

- **Reframe Negative Thoughts:** When self-doubt arises, it's essential to challenge and reframe negative thoughts. This involves questioning the validity of our self-doubt and replacing negative thoughts with more balanced and affirming perspectives. For example, if the inner critic says, "I'm not good enough," one can challenge this thought by asking, "What evidence supports this belief, and what evidence contradicts it?"

- **Practice Self-Compassion:** Developing self-compassion is essential for challenging self-doubt. Instead of being self-critical, individuals can cultivate a kind and understanding attitude toward themselves, acknowledging that self-doubt is a natural human experience. By treating oneself with the same kindness and empathy that one would offer a friend, individuals can counteract the impact of self-doubt.

- **Seek Support:** Building a support network of trusted friends, family members, affiliated spiritual and religious support groups, or mental health professionals can provide valuable perspectives and encouragement when facing self-doubt. Seeking the input of others can help challenge distorted self-perceptions and offer reassurance, validation, and feedback to counteract self-doubt.

- **Set Realistic Goals:** Unrealistic expectations and goals can often fuel self-doubt. Individuals can build confidence and reinforce a positive self-image by setting achievable and realistic goals. Celebrating small victories and progress can counteract the influence of self-doubt and foster a sense of accomplishment.

- **Challenge Perfectionism:** Perfectionism often underlies self-doubt as individuals strive for unattainable standards. Challenging the need for perfection and embracing growth, mistakes, and imperfections can help individuals break free from the grip of self-doubt.

- **Focus on Strengths and Accomplishments:** Practicing gratitude and acknowledging personal strengths and achievements can help shift the focus away from self-doubt. By recognizing past successes and positive attributes, individuals can build a more balanced and affirming self-perception.

- **Try Scriptural Meditation:** Replacing negative thoughts with God's truth is invaluable to breaking free from self-doubt. When negative self-talk arises, consciously replace it with positive affirmation rooted in scripture. Instead of saying, "I'm not good enough," declare, "I am fearfully and wonderfully made" (Psalm 139:14). Rather than thinking, "I'll never succeed," affirm, "I can do all things through Christ, who strengthens me" (Philippians 4:13).

Meditate on these truths until they become ingrained in your mind and heart.

As we conclude our exploration of understanding self-doubt and unmasking the inner critic, it's clear that recognizing and challenging self-doubt is an essential step toward fostering self-compassion and building resilience. By gaining insight into the origins of self-doubt and implementing strategies to challenge it, individuals can take proactive steps toward developing a more empowered and confident sense of self.

In the next chapter, we explore the transformative journey of building a strong foundation through self-acceptance and authenticity, offering guidance on embracing one's true self and cultivating a more positive and authentic way of being.

I praise you because I am fearfully and wonderfully made; your works are wonderful, I know that full well. – **Psalm 139:14**

Chapter 2:

Building a Strong Foundation: Self-Acceptance and Authenticity

Self-acceptance and authenticity are two fundamental aspects of personal growth and well-being. In the modern world, where social media often portrays perfection and constantly pushes unrealistic standards, it is crucial to understand the importance of embracing imperfections and being true to oneself. This chapter explores the significance of building a strong foundation by cultivating self-acceptance and authenticity and how these qualities contribute to living a fulfilled and meaningful life.

Embracing Imperfections

In a world that often idolizes flawlessness, embracing imperfections can be challenging. However, it is essential to recognize that imperfections are part of what makes each individual unique. Embracing imperfections involves acknowledging and accepting one's flaws, mistakes, and limitations without judgment or self-criticism. This process of self-compassion and acceptance allows individuals to let go of the pressures of perfection and instead focus on their strengths and inner qualities.

The scripture above beautifully articulates the concept of embracing imperfections. The verse emphasizes the idea that every individual is uniquely created and inherently valuable. It encourages self-appreciation and recognition of the wonder in one's own creation, which aligns with the notion of embracing imperfections.

Corroborating this with the chapter's theme, it underscores the importance of acknowledging one's intrinsic worth and embracing imperfections as an integral part of the self. A strong foundation of self-acceptance is built upon this understanding, enabling individuals to cultivate a positive self-image and genuine self-love.

Self-Acceptance and Authenticity

Self-acceptance goes hand in hand with authenticity (*The Power of Authenticity*, 2023). Being authentic means staying true to oneself, being honest about one's feelings, and aligning actions with personal values and beliefs. It involves embracing one's true identity and rejecting societal pressures to conform to idealized standards. Authenticity fosters genuine connections with others and cultivates a sense of inner peace and confidence.

The verse from Psalm 139:14 further reinforces the importance of self-acceptance and authenticity by highlighting the divine intention behind each individual's creation. It encourages individuals to recognize and appreciate their unique qualities and to live authentically in accordance with their true selves. This aligns with the chapter's emphasis on building a solid foundation based on self-acceptance and authenticity.

In today's society, where external validation and societal norms can overshadow individual authenticity, it becomes increasingly vital to internalize the wisdom found in this scripture. By recognizing the intrinsic value placed upon each individual and embracing imperfections as a normal part of life, one can lay the groundwork for a life grounded in self-acceptance and authenticity.

Cultivating Self-Compassion

Cultivating self-compassion is vital to building a foundation of self-acceptance and authenticity. It involves treating oneself with kindness, understanding, and empathy, particularly in times of difficulties, failures, or self-perceived flaws. By developing self-compassion, individuals can cultivate a healthier relationship with themselves and foster a more positive self-image.

Self-compassion requires individuals to recognize their own suffering and extend the same level of compassion toward themselves as they would to a loved one. It involves acknowledging one's pain or shortcomings without judgment or self-criticism. This practice allows individuals to navigate challenging situations with a sense of understanding and kindness rather than falling into a spiral of self-blame or self-doubt.

In the context of building a strong foundation, self-compassion provides individuals with a secure and stable base from which they can explore their authentic selves. It is a necessary tool for navigating the complexities of self-acceptance and allows individuals to embrace their imperfections without diminishing their self-worth. Through self-compassion, individuals can cultivate a greater sense of self-acceptance by acknowledging that their flaws and mistakes are part of their human experience rather than defining factors that diminish their value.

Research has shown that self-compassionate individuals are more resilient and have higher levels of psychological well-being. They tend to have a more positive outlook on life and are better equipped to cope with stress and setbacks. By cultivating self-compassion, individuals create a nurturing and supportive internal environment that fosters self-acceptance, personal growth, and emotional well-being.

One scripture passage that resonates with the concept of self-compassion is Colossians 3:12: "Therefore, as God's chosen people, holy and dearly loved, clothe yourselves with compassion, kindness, humility, gentleness, and patience." This verse highlights the importance of extending compassion not only to others but also to oneself. It emphasizes that individuals are chosen and loved by a higher power, affirming their inherent worth and encouraging them to treat themselves with kindness and compassion.

Honoring Your Unique Self

Honoring your unique self is an essential aspect of cultivating self-acceptance and authenticity. It involves recognizing and embracing your individuality, strengths, weaknesses, quirks, and characteristics that make you distinctly you. By honoring your unique self, you acknowledge your inherent worth and value, leading to a more profound sense of self-acceptance and authenticity.

Embracing your uniqueness means celebrating the qualities that set you apart from others. Instead of trying to fit into societal norms or conform to external expectations, honoring your unique self involves staying true to your authentic identity and expressing yourself honestly and genuinely. This process of self-recognition and acceptance allows you to embrace your strengths, talents, and personal attributes without fear of judgment or comparison.

Honoring your unique self aligns with self-acceptance and authenticity by encouraging individuals to live according to their true selves. By recognizing and valuing your unique qualities, you cultivate a sense of self-respect and self-appreciation, forming a strong foundation for personal growth and well-being.

By honoring your unique self, you embrace your individuality, strengths, and imperfections with love and acceptance. This process fosters a deeper connection with yourself and allows you to live authentically, in alignment with your values, beliefs, and true identity. Honoring your unique self empowers you to embrace your authenticity, express yourself with confidence, and cultivate a sense of inner peace and fulfillment.

In conclusion, building a solid foundation through self-acceptance and authenticity is a transformative journey that leads to personal empowerment and fulfillment. Embracing imperfections, cultivating self-compassion, and honoring one's unique self are essential for establishing this foundation. By integrating these principles into daily life, individuals can embark on a path of self-discovery, self-compassion, and genuine connection with themselves and others. This chapter has served as a guiding light for those seeking to cultivate a deep sense of self-acceptance and authenticity, ultimately leading to a more meaningful and purposeful existence.

In the next chapter, we will explore the concept of mindset and examine the differences between fixed and growth mindsets. We discuss the power of adopting a growth mindset and the strategies for shifting from a fixed mindset to a growth mindset. By understanding and embracing the principles of a growth mindset, individuals can overcome challenges, embrace learning and development, and experience a profound mindset makeover that can positively impact all areas of life.

Do not conform to the pattern of this world, but be transformed by the renewing of your mind. –Romans 12:2

Chapter 3:

Mindset Makeover: Shifting From Fixed to Growth Mindset

In our journey toward personal growth and self-improvement, our mindset is one of the most fundamental aspects to address. Our mindset, beliefs, and attitudes we hold about ourselves and our abilities profoundly impact how we approach challenges and handle setbacks and, ultimately, determine our success and happiness in life.

A growth mindset is the belief that one's abilities and intelligence can be developed and strengthened over time through dedication, hard work, and perseverance. Those with a growth mindset embrace challenges, view failures as opportunities for learning and improvement, and are open to constructive feedback.

On the other hand, a fixed mindset is characterized by the belief that one's abilities and intelligence are innate and static, leading individuals to perceive their talents and skills as predetermined and unchangeable. Those with a fixed mindset may avoid challenges for fear of failure, view setbacks as a reflection of their inherent limitations, and may resist feedback or constructive criticism. In this chapter, we will explore the concepts of fixed and growth mindsets and understand the power of shifting from a fixed mindset to a growth mindset.

The Power of Shifting From Fixed to Growth Mindset

The impact of our mindset on our lives is significant, affecting various aspects of our personal and professional development (Dice, 2024). By shifting from a fixed mindset to a growth mindset, we open ourselves up to a world of possibilities and opportunities for transformation. Here's how the power of shifting from a fixed to a growth mindset can make a positive difference in our lives:

- **Embracing Challenges:** Individuals with a growth mindset see challenges as opportunities for growth and learning. They understand that they can overcome obstacles and develop new skills through effort and perseverance. Instead of avoiding challenges, they seek them out, knowing that it is through challenges that true growth occurs.

- **Developing Resilience:** A growth mindset fosters resilience in the face of setbacks and failures. Individuals with a growth mindset perceive setbacks as temporary and view them as learning experiences. They bounce back from failures, adjust their strategies, and use setbacks as stepping stones toward further growth and improvement.

- **Cultivating a Love for Learning:** With a growth mindset, individuals develop a passion for learning. They understand that continuous learning and effort can develop intelligence and abilities. This mindset fuels a thirst for knowledge, encouraging individuals to seek new experiences, acquire new skills, and expand their understanding of the world.

- **Building Self-Confidence:** Shifting to a growth mindset enhances self-confidence. Individuals with a growth mindset believe in their ability to learn and improve. They recognize that their efforts and dedication can lead to tangible progress and success. This self-belief drives them to take on new challenges, persevere through difficulties, and ultimately achieve their goals.

- **Nurturing a Positive Mindset:** A growth mindset leads to a more positive overall outlook on life. By embracing challenges, learning from setbacks, and never giving up on effort, individuals with a growth mindset approach life with optimism and hope. They see difficulties as opportunities for growth and setbacks as temporary detours on their journey towards success.

Techniques to Foster a Growth-Oriented Mindset

To cultivate a growth-oriented mindset, it is essential to actively engage in practices and techniques that encourage a positive and adaptive approach to learning, challenges, and personal development. By incorporating the following techniques into daily life, individuals can foster a mindset that embraces growth, resilience, and a passion for continuous improvement:

- **Explore New Experiences:** Rather than shying away from challenges, make it a point to seek out new experiences and opportunities that push you out of your comfort zone. This will allow you to develop new skills, learn from experiences, and expand your capabilities, contributing to a growth-oriented mindset.

- **Cultivate a "Yet" Mentality:** Adopt the power of "yet" to reframe your beliefs about your abilities. Instead of saying, "I can't do this," add "yet" to the statement, shifting your mindset to see capabilities as works in progress rather than fixed traits. For example, "I can't do this... yet."

- **Learn From Setbacks:** Instead of viewing setbacks as failures, see them as learning opportunities. Reflect on the lessons gained from setbacks, adjust your strategies, and use the experience to grow and improve. This approach fosters resilience and a growth mindset.

- **Practice Positive Self-Talk**: Monitor your self-talk and challenge negative, self-limiting beliefs. Replace self-criticism with affirmations that reinforce your potential for growth and learning. You can shift your mindset toward a more optimistic and growth-oriented perspective by cultivating a positive internal dialogue.

- **Focus on Effort and Progress:** Shift the emphasis from outcomes to the process of learning and improvement. Celebrate efforts, progress, and achievements along the way, recognizing that growth is a journey rather than a destination. Valuing the process fosters a mindset focused on continuous learning and development.

- **Seek Constructive Feedback:** Embrace feedback as a valuable source of learning and growth. Actively seek out constructive criticism and use it as a tool for improvement. Being open to feedback and using it to refine your skills and approaches contributes to a growth-oriented mindset.

- **Adopt a Curiosity Mindset:** Nurture a sense of curiosity and a thirst for knowledge. Approach new experiences with an open mind, ask questions, and explore new perspectives. Embracing curiosity enhances your capacity for learning and fuels a growth-oriented mindset.

- **Set Learning Goals:** Establish specific, achievable goals that focus on learning and personal development. By setting goals related to acquiring new skills or expanding your knowledge, you create a framework for continuous growth and improvement.

- **Surround Yourself With Growth Mindset Advocates:** Engage with individuals who embody a growth-oriented mindset. Surrounding yourself with people who prioritize learning, resilience, and personal development can inspire and reinforce your own growth-oriented perspective.

- **Reflect on Growth:** Take time to reflect on your personal and professional growth journey. Acknowledge your progress, identify areas for further development, and celebrate your commitment to continuous learning and improvement.

Overcoming Limiting Beliefs

Limiting beliefs are deeply ingrained thoughts and attitudes that constrain our lives, hinder our potential, and prevent us from reaching our goals. These beliefs often stem from negative experiences, societal conditioning, or self-doubt and can significantly impact our mindset and behavior. Overcoming limiting beliefs is essential for personal growth, self-improvement, and success. Here are some strategies to effectively address and overcome limiting beliefs:

- **Identify and Challenge Limiting Beliefs:** The first step in overcoming limiting beliefs is identifying them. Reflect on your thoughts, fears, and self-doubts, and pinpoint the beliefs that are holding you back. Once identified, challenge these beliefs by questioning their validity and examining the evidence that supports or refutes them.

- **Reframe Negative Self-Talk:** Limiting beliefs often manifest as negative self-talk, such as "I'm not good enough," "I can't do this," or "I'm not worthy." Reframe these negative statements into empowering affirmations that promote self-confidence and a growth mindset. For example, "I am capable of overcoming challenges," "I have the skills and resilience to succeed," or "I am deserving of success."

- **Explore the Origins of Limiting Beliefs:** Explore the origins of your limiting beliefs to gain insight into how they were formed. Understanding the root causes of these beliefs, whether from childhood experiences, societal influences, or personal setbacks, can help you challenge and reframe them from a place of awareness and understanding.

- **Seek Evidence to Dispute Limiting Beliefs:** Gather evidence that contradicts your limiting beliefs and supports a more empowered mindset. Look for examples of your past successes, positive feedback from others, or instances where you demonstrated the qualities or abilities you believe you lack. Building a case against your limiting beliefs can weaken their hold on your mindset.

- **Visualize Success and Empowerment:** Engage in visualization exercises that depict yourself overcoming challenges, achieving your goals, and embodying empowerment. Visualization can help reprogram your subconscious mind, counteracting limiting beliefs with positive, empowering images and emotions.

- **Embrace Self-Compassion:** Be kind and compassionate towards yourself as you work to overcome limiting beliefs. Recognize that these beliefs are deeply rooted and may take time to address. Practice self-compassion by replacing self-criticism with self-acceptance and understanding.

- **Surround Yourself With Empowering Influences:** Seek out individuals, resources, and environments that foster empowerment, positivity, and a growth-oriented mindset. Engage with supportive friends, mentors, or communities that encourage personal development and challenge limiting beliefs.

- **Take Incremental Steps Outside Your Comfort Zone:** Gradually expose yourself to situations that challenge your limiting beliefs. By taking small, calculated risks and pushing beyond your comfort zone, you can build confidence and prove to yourself that your limiting beliefs are unfounded.

- **Embrace a Growth Mindset:** Cultivate a growth-oriented mindset that sees challenges, setbacks, and failures as opportunities for learning and growth. Focus on continuous improvement, resilience, and a belief in your ability to develop and adapt.

- **Seek Professional Support if Needed:** If limiting beliefs significantly impact your well-being and hinder your ability to function, consider seeking professional support from a therapist, counselor, spiritual director, pastor, or life coach. Professional guidance can provide valuable insights and effective strategies for overcoming limiting beliefs.

As the sun sets on our exploration of shifting from a fixed to a growth mindset, remember that change is not always easy, but with persistence and effort, we can transform our beliefs and unleash our true potential. Embrace the journey ahead with an open mind and a willingness to learn and grow.

In the next chapter, we will look into building our very own confidence toolbox—a collection of skills and habits that will empower us to step into our full potential and radiate with self-assurance. From mastering the art of self-talk to cultivating a resilient mindset, this chapter will equip you with the essential tools needed to boost your confidence and conquer any challenge that comes your way.

For the Lord will be your confidence and will keep your foot from being caught. –Proverbs 3:26

Chapter 4:

The Confidence Toolbox:

Skills and Habits for

Confidence

In the journey of personal development and self-improvement, confidence is one of the most sought-after qualities. Confidence is not about appearing self-assured on the outside; it is about believing in oneself, trusting one's abilities, and facing challenges with resilience and positivity. Building confidence goes beyond superficial appearances; it requires a deep-rooted belief in one's worth and capabilities.

The Power of Effective Communication

Effective communication is one of the key pillars of confidence (Reierson, 2023). The way we express ourselves, both verbally and nonverbally, plays a significant role in how others perceive us and how we perceive ourselves. Effective communication is not only about speaking with clarity and articulation; it is also about listening actively, understanding others' perspectives, and expressing empathy and understanding.

In the context of confidence, effective communication is a powerful tool that can help us convey our thoughts, emotions, and ideas with clarity and confidence. When we communicate effectively, we build trust and rapport with others, foster healthy relationships, and create a positive impact on our personal and professional lives.

The scriptural passage from Proverbs 3:26 reminds us that true confidence comes from a place of faith and trust in God. When we surrender ourselves to the guidance and direction of the Divine, we can walk with confidence, knowing that we are supported and guided in every step we take. This passage emphasizes the importance of faith and reliance on a higher power as the foundation of true confidence.

Cultivating Confidence Through Communication Skills

Effective communication is not just about speaking; it also involves active listening, empathy, and nonverbal cues. When we listen attentively to others, we show respect and consideration, enhancing our interpersonal relationships and building trust. Empathy allows us to connect with others on a deeper level, showing understanding and compassion.

Nonverbal cues, such as body language, facial expressions, and tone of voice, also play a crucial role in communication. When we are aware of our nonverbal communication, we can convey confidence and assertiveness through our posture, gestures, and eye contact. Being mindful of our nonverbal cues can help us project a positive and confident image to others.

Assertiveness Training

Assertiveness training is essential in developing the skills and confidence needed to express ourselves effectively in personal and professional situations. Through assertiveness training, we learn to communicate our needs, feelings, and opinions confidently while also being mindful of the feelings of others.

Developing assertiveness skills requires a combination of self-awareness, communication skills, and confidence-building practices. Self-awareness allows us to recognize the situations that trigger passive or aggressive communication styles and identify areas for improvement. Communication skills such as active listening, empathy, and effective feedback can help us communicate assertively while building trust and rapport with others.

Confidence-building practices such as daily affirmations, visualization exercises, and positive self-talk can help boost our confidence and reinforce our belief in our abilities. These practices can help replace negative self-talk and limiting beliefs with positive affirmations and a growth mindset, which can enhance our assertiveness and communication skills.

Assertiveness training can be beneficial in various personal and professional situations, such as:

- **Negotiations:** Assertiveness skills are essential for negotiations in which we need to communicate our needs and opinions while respecting the needs of others.

- **Conflict Resolution:** Assertiveness skills can help us express our concerns and emotions confidently while seeking to resolve conflicts respectfully and effectively.

- **Interpersonal Relationships:** Assertiveness skills can help us set boundaries, communicate our needs, and build healthy relationships based on mutual respect and understanding.

- **Leadership:** Assertiveness skills are crucial for effective leadership, where clear communication, delegation, and management skills are essential.

Body Language and Posture

Body language and posture play a significant role in effective communication and projecting confidence. Our nonverbal cues, including body movements, facial expressions, and posture, can convey messages and emotions that often speak louder than words. Being aware of and intentionally managing our body language and posture can significantly enhance our communication and create a positive impression on others.

- **Facial Expressions:** Our facial expressions can communicate a range of emotions, including happiness, surprise, anger, or sadness. Smiling, making eye contact, and maintaining a relaxed, open facial expression can help convey approachability, warmth, and confidence. Avoiding expressions that convey discomfort, boredom, or disinterest is essential when trying to project confidence.

- **Eye Contact:** Maintaining appropriate eye contact is crucial for effective communication. It shows interest, attentiveness, and confidence. Direct eye contact helps establish a connection with others, conveys sincerity, and shows that you are actively engaged in the conversation. However, it's also important to strike a balance and not make continuous intense eye contact, which can come across as aggressive or intimidating.

- **Posture:** Your posture speaks volumes about your confidence level. Standing or sitting up straight with your shoulders back signals confidence and assertiveness. Slouching or hunching over can convey insecurity or lack of self-assurance. Good posture not only makes you appear more confident but can also improve your breathing and overall physical well-being.

- **Gestures:** Purposeful and controlled gestures can enhance communication and display confidence. Using appropriate hand gestures while expressing yourself can add emphasis and clarity to your words, making your message more engaging. However, wild or excessive gestures can be distracting and may undermine your credibility.

- **Personal Space:** Respecting personal space is crucial for effective communication and projecting confidence. Being too close to someone can make them feel uncomfortable or threatened, while standing too far away can create a sense of disinterest or detachment. Understanding and respecting cultural norms and personal boundaries is crucial in maintaining a comfortable and confident communication environment.

- **Mirroring and Reflecting:** Practicing and observing your body language and posture in front of a mirror can help you become more aware of your non-verbal cues. Pay attention to any unintentional habits or gestures you might have, and work on correcting them. Additionally, reflecting on past interactions or seeking feedback from others can help identify any areas for improvement and give you a clearer understanding of how others perceive your body language and posture.

Confidence is essential to personal growth and self-improvement, and effective communication is a critical tool for building confidence. By incorporating the skills and habits outlined in the Confidence Toolbox, we can cultivate our communication and assertiveness skills and enhance our self-belief and resilience. With practice and commitment, we can transform our personal and professional relationships and walk confidently, guided by faith and self-assurance.

In the next chapter, we will explore the importance of self-care and well-being in our personal and professional lives. Just as plants need nurturing, care, and attention to thrive, so do we require self-care practices to cultivate our physical, emotional, and mental well-being.

Do you not know that your bodies are temples of the Holy Spirit? –1 Corinthians 6:19–20

Chapter 5:

Self-Care and Well-Being: Nurturing Your Inner Garden

In today's fast-paced world, self-care and well-being have become essential to maintaining a healthy and balanced life. Just like tending to a garden requires time, effort, and dedication, nurturing our inner selves through self-care is crucial for our overall physical and mental health.

The scripture passage above serves as a powerful reminder of the sacredness of our bodies and the responsibility we have to care for them. By viewing our bodies as temples of the Holy Spirit, we are encouraged to treat ourselves with reverence and respect.

This perspective aligns with the concept of self-care, emphasizing the significance of nurturing our bodies as vessels that house divine energy and essence. This chapter explores the importance of self-care and its direct impact on our well-being, focusing on how taking care of our physical health influences our confidence and mental state.

Mental and Emotional Well-Being

Mental well-being encompasses our cognitive and psychological states, including our thoughts, perceptions, and overall mental health (Gautam et al., 2024). When we prioritize mental well-being, we cultivate resilience, clarity of mind, and emotional equilibrium.

Practices such as mindfulness meditation, cognitive reframing, and seeking professional and spiritual support when needed are crucial for nurturing mental well-being. By tending to our mental health, we honor the sanctity of our inner selves as temples of the Holy Spirit.

Emotional well-being involves our capacity to understand, express, and manage our emotions in a healthy and balanced manner. Cultivating emotional well-being involves fostering self-awareness, nurturing positive relationships, and developing coping strategies for stress and challenges. When we honor our emotional well-being, we acknowledge the sacred nature of our emotional experiences and seek to create an inner environment conducive to the presence of the Holy Spirit.

Prioritizing Self-Care Routines

Self-care routines nourish the soul by providing moments of rest, rejuvenation, and reflection amid life's demands. By prioritizing self-care rituals, we acknowledge our value and worth as individuals deserving of love and care. These rituals can take various forms, such as mindfulness practices, journaling, creative activities, or engaging in hobbies that bring us joy.

By honoring ourselves as temples of the Holy Spirit and prioritizing self-care routines, we create a nurturing space for inner growth, resilience, and connection to the divine within us. As we tend to our inner gardens with love, mindfulness, and intention, we nourish the seeds of wholeness and well-being that flourish within us, promoting a sense of balance, harmony, and vitality in body, mind, and spirit.

The next chapter will explore the power of courage in overcoming obstacles, pursuing our dreams, and embracing growth opportunities. By confronting our fears with bravery and taking bold steps toward our aspirations, we open ourselves up to new possibilities, resilience, and personal empowerment.

Though an army may encamp against me, my heart shall not fear. —Psalm 27:3

Chapter 6:

Facing Fear and Taking

Risks: Courageous Steps

Fear is a potent force that can hold us back from reaching our full potential and embracing new opportunities. It manifests in various ways, guiding our decisions and actions, often unconsciously. However, by understanding and identifying fear-based behaviors, we can begin to confront and overcome them. In this chapter, we will explore the power of courage in transcending fear, pursuing our dreams, and embracing personal growth. Drawing inspiration from the scriptural passage in Psalm 27:3, we seek to align our thoughts with divine teachings as we embark on a journey of courage and risk-taking.

Gradual Exposure to Discomfort

Gradual exposure to discomfort is a technique commonly used in cognitive behavioral therapy (CBT) to help individuals overcome fear and anxiety (*What Is Exposure Therapy?* 2022). It involves systematically and gradually exposing oneself to situations or stimuli that trigger fear or discomfort. The purpose of this approach is to desensitize the individual to their fears and build resilience, leading to a reduction in anxiety and an increased ability to face challenging situations.

The principle behind gradual exposure is based on the idea that fear and anxiety are learned responses that can be unlearned through repeated exposure. By confronting feared situations in a controlled and gradual manner, individuals can gradually decrease their fear response and develop a sense of mastery and confidence.

The process of gradual exposure begins with identifying the specific fear or anxiety-triggering situation or stimuli. It is important to be as specific as possible, as this allows for more focused and effective exposure. For example, suppose someone has a fear of public speaking. In that case, the focus may be on gradually exposing themselves to speaking in front of small groups and then gradually increasing the size of the audience.

Exposure can take different forms depending on the nature of the fear. It can involve imaginal exposure, where the individual mentally imagines themselves in the feared situation, or exposure, where the individual physically exposes themselves to the feared situation. For example, someone who fears flying may start by looking at pictures of airplanes, then progress to watching videos of flights, and eventually work up to taking short flights.

Celebrating Small Victories

The concept of celebrating small victories is rooted in the idea of positive reinforcement and self-encouragement. By acknowledging and celebrating even the smallest steps toward our goals, we can boost our confidence, motivation, and sense of accomplishment. These moments of triumph, no matter how insignificant they may appear in the grand scheme of things, are powerful reminders of our progress and perseverance.

Moreover, celebrating small victories helps cultivate a mindset of gratitude and appreciation for the journey itself. We often get so caught up in pursuing our long-term objectives that we overlook the smaller moments of success that occur along the way. By taking the time to pause, reflect, and savor these little wins, we can gain a deeper appreciation for the effort and dedication we have invested in our endeavors.

Incorporating the principle of celebrating small victories into our daily lives can lead to a more positive and empowered mindset. It fosters a sense of self-confidence, instills a greater sense of self-worth, and reinforces the belief that we can overcome obstacles and achieve our goals. By building a habit of acknowledging and celebrating our accomplishments, we can create a cycle of success that fuels our momentum and propels us toward more significant achievements.

As we conclude this chapter, it's essential to recognize that pursuing personal growth and self-improvement is not without its challenges. Conquering fear and embracing risk requires a steadfast commitment to courage, resilience, and self-discovery. By fostering an unwavering determination to confront our fears and venture into the unknown, we can unlock new opportunities and possibilities for growth.

The next chapter explores the intricacies of developing the social skills and mindset needed to thrive in diverse social settings. By honing our ability to communicate effectively, exude confidence, and build authentic connections, we can enhance our social interactions and create positive, lasting impressions in both personal and professional spheres.

There is no fear in love. But perfect love drives out fear. –1 John 4:18

Chapter 7:

Social Confidence:

Navigating Social

Situations

Social anxiety, characterized by an overwhelming fear of judgment, embarrassment, or rejection in social settings, can hinder one's ability to fully engage and connect with others. The fear of saying the wrong thing, being perceived negatively, or feeling inadequate can create a barrier that limits one's social interactions and inhibits the development of meaningful relationships. This fear and self-doubt can manifest in physical symptoms such as rapid heartbeat, sweating, trembling, and a sense of dread, further exacerbating the anxiety surrounding social situations.

To address social anxiety and build social confidence, it is essential to unpack the underlying beliefs, thoughts, and emotions that contribute to this sense of unease. By exploring the root causes of one's fears and examining the negative self-talk and limiting beliefs that fuel social anxiety, individuals can begin to challenge and reframe their perceptions of themselves and others.

This process of self-awareness and cognitive restructuring lays the foundation for building resilience, enhancing self-esteem, and fostering a more positive and empowering mindset when navigating social interactions.

The scripture passage from 1 John 4:18 provides a profound reflection on the relationship between fear and love in the context of social confidence. The verse speaks about the transformative power of love, compassion, and acceptance in overcoming fear and anxiety. By cultivating a deep sense of self-love, acceptance, and empathy towards oneself and others, individuals can free themselves from the shackles of fear and embrace social interactions with confidence and authenticity.

Building Meaningful Connections

Building meaningful connections can sometimes feel like a daunting task in a world where we are constantly connected through technology. The ability to form deep, authentic relationships is essential for our social and emotional well-being. Yet, it can be challenging to know how to connect with others in a meaningful way.

Building meaningful connections involves more than small talk and surface-level interactions. Meaningful connections are built through vulnerability, empathy, and mutual respect. They require individuals to show up authentically, share their genuine selves, and hold space for others to do the same.

When individuals aim to build meaningful connections, they must first identify their values and beliefs. By understanding what matters to them, individuals can find others who share similar values and interests. When individuals connect with others who share their passions, it becomes easier to form a bond that extends beyond surface-level interactions.

Networking and Relationship-Building

Networking is often associated with professional contexts, where individuals actively seek to expand their circle of contacts for career advancement, business opportunities, and professional growth. Networking involves strategic outreach, often within specific industries or fields, to form mutually beneficial connections. Key elements of effective networking include establishing a strong professional presence, engaging in industry events and gatherings, and initiating conversations that create opportunities for collaboration and advancement.

On the other hand, relationship-building encompasses a broader, more holistic approach to connecting with others. It transcends professional objectives and extends into personal and community spheres. Relationship-building emphasizes the development of genuine, long-term connections based on trust, empathy, and mutual support. Unlike networking, relationship-building focuses on creating meaningful bonds that extend beyond immediate gains and transactions.

By embracing a mindset of authenticity, empathy, and self-acceptance, individuals can navigate social situations with grace, cultivate meaningful connections, and embark on a journey toward greater confidence and connection.

As we transition to the next chapter, let us continue our quest for personal growth and self-discovery, exploring ways to nurture our self-worth and celebrate the unique value we bring to the world. Self-esteem is the cornerstone of our emotional well-being, shaping how we perceive ourselves and interact with the world around us. By embracing practices that celebrate our worth, foster self-compassion, and cultivate a positive self-image, we can enhance our confidence, resilience, and sense of fulfillment.

*For we are God's handiwork, created
in Christ Jesus to do good works. –*
Ephesians 2:10

Chapter 8:

Self-Esteem Boosters:

Celebrating Your Worth

Self-esteem is an essential aspect of human nature that is often downplayed or ignored. It refers to the value one places on oneself. Healthy self-esteem involves recognizing and accepting oneself for who you are, including strengths and weaknesses. Many factors, such as life events, societal pressures, and personal perceptions, can influence self-esteem. However, regardless of the factors affecting it, self-esteem is essential to overall well-being. This chapter focuses on how to boost one's self-esteem through affirmations and positive self-talk.

Affirmations involve repeatedly speaking positive statements about oneself to boost confidence and elevate self-esteem. Positive self-talk, on the other hand, is similar to affirmations, but it is spontaneous thoughts that affirm one's worth and potential. Both affirmations and positive self-talk are powerful tools for boosting self-esteem.

Astute observations suggest that we can build up our confidence and self-esteem by what we say to ourselves repeatedly. This is predominantly facilitated by affirmative statements that focus on our strengths and reinforce important self-concepts. This approach is considered a powerful tool embraced in various fields, ranging from education to therapy.

The interconnectivity between affirmations and cognitive restructuring can be understood accurately through the scriptural passage in Ephesians 2:10. It highlights individual worth and one's purpose as unique creations of God. The verse underscores individuality and the value of one's life. The underlying message is that individuals possess unique skills and abilities that can be used to fulfill their purpose. Such a message is relatable in the modern world, where one's value is often entangled in societal expectations and comparisons to others.

Recognizing Achievements

When individuals take the time to acknowledge and celebrate their accomplishments, it positively impacts their self-perception and overall well-being. Recognizing achievements reinforces one's capabilities and can significantly contribute to building and maintaining healthy self-esteem.

One of the fundamental benefits of recognizing achievements is that it provides a sense of validation and acknowledgment of one's efforts. This validation can be internal, through self-recognition, or external, through recognition from others. When individuals take the time to acknowledge their achievements, they reinforce a positive self-image, which can lead to increased confidence and a sense of pride in their abilities.

Moreover, recognizing achievements can act as a source of motivation. When individuals acknowledge their successes, no matter how big or small, it can drive them to pursue further goals and aspirations. It serves as a reminder of past accomplishments and the hard work that led to those successes, which can boost confidence and fuel the drive to continue progressing.

Additionally, celebrating achievements can contribute to a positive mindset. Individuals can cultivate a more optimistic outlook by focusing on the positive aspects of one's experiences and efforts. This can be especially impactful during challenging times, as reflecting on past achievements can be a source of resilience and hope.

Recognizing achievements also plays a role in fostering a growth mindset. When individuals take the time to acknowledge their progress and successes, it reinforces the belief that improvement and development are possible. This can lead to a willingness to take on new challenges and a sense of self-efficacy in overcoming obstacles.

In the context of the scriptural passage above, recognizing achievements aligns with the idea of being "created in Christ Jesus to do good works." When individuals recognize their achievements, they acknowledge the good works they have contributed, whether in their personal lives, relationships, professional endeavors, or community involvement. This recognition can serve as a reminder of the value and purpose of one's actions, contributing to a deeper sense of fulfillment and alignment with one's spiritual calling.

Gratitude Practices

Gratitude practices are essential for fostering a positive mindset and enhancing overall well-being. By focusing on what we are thankful for, we shift our attention from negativity and lack to abundance and appreciation. The simple act of expressing gratitude can lead to a profound transformation in our outlook on life, promoting feelings of contentment, joy, and fulfillment.

There are various ways to incorporate gratitude practices into our daily routines. Keeping a gratitude journal, where we write down things we are grateful for each day, can help us stay attuned to the blessings in our lives. Practicing mindfulness and expressing gratitude in the present moment can deepen our awareness of the goodness around us.

Incorporating gratitude into daily routines, such as praying before meals or reflecting on moments of kindness throughout the day, reinforces a spirit of thankfulness. Gratitude practices also have a ripple effect on our relationships, enhancing our connections with others and fostering a sense of community and reciprocity.

As we conclude this chapter on self-esteem boosters, it is crucial to remember that celebrating our worth is an ongoing practice. Affirmations, positive self-talk, and gratitude practices are just some of the tools we can use to nurture our self-esteem and cultivate a healthy sense of self-worth. By incorporating these practices into our daily lives, we can continue to grow and thrive in our journey toward self-acceptance and empowerment.

In the next chapter, we will explore the transformative power of embracing failure and developing resilience. Failure is an inevitable part of life, and how we respond to it can significantly impact our self-esteem, confidence, and overall well-being. By reframing our perspective on failure and cultivating resilience, we can learn to bounce back from setbacks with strength and determination.

And we know that in all things, God works for the good of those who love him. –Romans 8:28

Chapter 9:

Embracing Failure and Resilience: Bouncing Back Stronger

In the journey of life, failure is an inevitable part of the human experience. Despite our best efforts and intentions, setbacks and disappointments will occur. However, our response to these failures truly defines our character and shapes our future. This chapter looks into the transformative power of reframing failure as an opportunity for learning and growth, leading to greater resilience and the ability to bounce back stronger.

The scriptural passage from Romans 8:28 beautifully encapsulates the theme of embracing failure and resilience. The verse reminds us that despite adversity, there is a divine purpose at work. It speaks to the belief that God can turn our failures into opportunities for growth and blessings for those who remain faithful and love Him.

Developing Resilience Muscles

Resilience is the ability to adapt and bounce back from adversity, setbacks, or challenges. It is a crucial trait that allows individuals to face life's difficulties with strength and determination. This section explores the concept of developing resilience muscles, shedding light on the importance of actively cultivating resilience and providing practical strategies for doing so.

Practical Strategies for Developing Resilience

- **Cultivate a Positive Mindset:** A positive mindset is a foundational aspect of building resilience. By reframing challenges as opportunities for growth, individuals can develop a mindset that perceives setbacks as temporary and solvable rather than permanent obstacles.

- **Build Emotional Resilience:** Emotional resilience involves developing the ability to identify, understand, and manage emotions effectively. This can be achieved through mindfulness, self-reflection, and emotional regulation techniques.

- **Foster Supportive Relationships:** Building a strong support system is vital for resilience.

Surrounding oneself with positive and supportive individuals who can provide encouragement, guidance, and a listening ear can significantly contribute to one's ability to bounce back from setbacks.

- **Practice Self-Care:** Taking care of oneself physically, emotionally, and mentally is crucial for developing resilience muscles. Engaging in activities that promote well-being, such as exercise, meditation, hobbies, and quality sleep, enhances an individual's ability to cope with adversity and maintain a balanced perspective.

- **Learn From Failure:** Embracing failure as a learning opportunity is essential for resilience development. By reflecting on past failures, individuals can extract valuable lessons and apply them to future challenges. This helps them navigate setbacks with wisdom, flexibility, and a deeper understanding of their strengths and limitations.

Perseverance and Adaptability

Perseverance is the steadfast commitment to pursuing goals and overcoming obstacles despite difficulties, setbacks, or failures. It requires resilience, determination, and a strong belief in one's abilities and capacity for growth. Individuals who cultivate perseverance are better equipped to weather life's storms, maintain focus in the face of adversity, and ultimately achieve their desired outcomes.

Adaptability is the ability to adjust to new circumstances, challenges, or unexpected events with flexibility and resourcefulness. In a constantly evolving world that presents new challenges, adaptability is a crucial skill that allows individuals to thrive in complex and uncertain environments. By embracing change, being open to learning, and seeking innovative solutions, individuals can navigate transitions and setbacks with grace and resilience.

This chapter underscored the transformative power of failure as a teacher and resilience as a guiding force in navigating life's challenges. Through intentional practice, perseverance, and adaptability, individuals can develop the ability to face setbacks with courage, resilience, and a renewed sense of purpose. With these qualities as guiding principles, individuals are empowered to bounce back from adversity, thrive in the face of challenges, and embrace the journey of personal growth and self-discovery.

The next chapter explores the importance of developing and cultivating confidence as a lifelong practice. Confidence is not a fixed quality but a skill that can be nurtured and sustained through intentional habits and mindset shifts. By adopting empowering beliefs, practicing self-affirmation, setting achievable goals, and stepping outside comfort zones, individuals can strengthen their confidence muscles and cultivate a deep sense of self-assurance that serves as a foundation for personal growth and success.

*So do not throw away your
confidence; it will be richly rewarded.*
–Hebrews 10:35

Chapter 10:

Sustaining Confidence:

Lifelong Confidence Habits

Confidence is a quality that empowers individuals to believe in their abilities, navigate challenges with resilience, and pursue their goals with conviction. In this chapter, we will explore the profound impact of maintaining confidence as a lifelong practice. By exploring maintenance strategies, harnessing the power of positive thoughts, and drawing inspiration from scriptural wisdom, individuals can cultivate a deep sense of self-assurance that propels them toward success, fulfillment, and personal growth.

Maintenance Strategies for Sustaining Confidence

Maintaining confidence as a lifelong habit requires intentional effort, self-awareness, and a commitment to personal growth. By incorporating the following strategies into daily practices, individuals can strengthen their confidence muscles and cultivate a sense of self-assurance that withstands challenges and uncertainties:

- **Self-Affirmation:** Engage in positive self-talk and affirmations to reinforce beliefs in your abilities, strengths, and potential for success. Repeat affirmations such as "I am capable; I am resilient; I am worthy" to boost self-confidence and mitigate self-doubt.

- **Goal-Setting:** Establish clear, achievable goals that align with your values and aspirations. Setting specific, measurable objectives provides a road map for progress, instills a sense of purpose, and bolsters confidence in your ability to pursue and achieve your dreams.

- **Continuous Learning:** Embrace opportunities for growth, learning, and skill development. Expanding your knowledge, acquiring new skills, and challenging yourself to step outside your comfort zone fosters confidence by demonstrating your capacity for growth and adaptability.

- **Seeking Support:** Surround yourself with a supportive network of friends, mentors, and allies who uplift, encourage, and empower you. Seek feedback, guidance, and encouragement from those who believe in your potential and inspire you to reach new heights of confidence and accomplishment.

- **Practicing Resilience:** Embrace setbacks, failures, and challenges as opportunities for learning and growth. Resilience is the bedrock of confidence, enabling individuals to bounce back stronger, wiser, and more determined to pursue their goals and dreams.

The scriptural passage in Hebrews 10:35 provides inspiration and guidance for individuals seeking to sustain their confidence amidst trials and tribulations. The verse reminds us not to waver in our belief in ourselves and our abilities, for confidence is a virtue that will be richly rewarded. By anchoring ourselves in faith, perseverance, and unwavering belief in our potential, we can navigate challenges with resilience, pursue our goals with conviction, and trust that our confidence will be met with abundant blessings and rewards.

Accountability and Support

Accountability refers to taking responsibility for our actions, goals, and commitments. It involves being answerable to oneself and others, which can be highly beneficial in maintaining confidence. By setting clear objectives and regularly evaluating our progress, we hold ourselves accountable for our actions and choices.

This sense of responsibility fosters a sense of self-assurance as we actively work towards our goals.

Moreover, seeking external support is equally important in the journey of sustaining confidence. Surrounding ourselves with a supportive network of friends, family, mentors, or professionals can provide encouragement, guidance, and reassurance. These individuals can serve as sounding boards for our ideas, offer constructive feedback, and provide emotional support during challenging times. Their belief in our abilities and willingness to support us can bolster our confidence and inspire us to keep striving for success.

The Journey Toward Lasting Confidence

The path to lasting confidence begins with self-awareness and self-acceptance. Understanding our strengths, weaknesses, and values is essential to build a solid foundation for confidence. Embracing our uniqueness and imperfections allows us to develop a positive self-image and inner strength. Furthermore, the journey toward lasting confidence involves overcoming challenges and setbacks with resilience and determination. Adversity often tests our confidence, but we can strengthen our belief in ourselves by embracing failures as learning opportunities and persisting in the face of obstacles.

As we conclude this chapter, it is evident that the journey toward lasting confidence is multifaceted. By embracing the maintenance strategies, accountability, support, and the profound understanding that confidence is not static but a continuously nurtured quality, we pave the way for unwavering self-assurance. The wisdom shared in this chapter is a guiding light for cultivating habits and mindsets that will sustain our confidence throughout our lives.

Conclusion

In the journey through *Confidence Rx*, we have explored the depths of confidence, unraveling the essence of self-assurance and its profound impact on our lives. As we reach the culmination of this transformative exploration, it is essential to reflect on the key takeaways that have fortified our understanding and empowered our pursuit of confidence.

Throughout the chapters, we have learned that confidence is not merely a fleeting feeling but a dynamic quality that can be cultivated, nurtured, and sustained. By embracing self-awareness, self-compassion, and a growth mindset, we lay the groundwork for enduring confidence that withstands life's trials.

The invaluable teachings from biblical scriptures have illuminated the spiritual dimensions of confidence, emphasizing the role of faith, resilience, and divine strength in nurturing our self-belief.

Moreover, the practical strategies and exercises presented in this book have equipped us with the tools to navigate the complexities of confidence, fostering accountability, support systems, and lifelong habits that fortify our self-assurance.

As you embark on the journey to implement the strategies and insights shared in this book, remember that transformation is a process, and having the proper support can make all the difference. If you're seeking personalized guidance, accountability, or mentorship, I am here to help you achieve your goals. Feel free to reach out to me for 1-on-1 coaching or mentoring. Together, we can create a tailored plan that aligns with your unique aspirations and challenges, ensuring you stay on track and motivated.

You can connect with me via:

- Email: mistufemgroupllc@gmail.com

- Website: www.mistufemgroup.com

I look forward to working with you and supporting your journey toward a more empowered and confident life. Thank you for allowing me to be a part of your growth and transformation.

With gratitude,

Femi Olaseni, MSc, MDiv, Chaplain, and Coach

References

Dice, J. K. (2024, January 2). *The impact of mindset on personal and professional growth*. Mind Shift Works. https://mindshift.works/the-impact-of-mindset-on-personal-and-professional-growth/

Gautam, S., Jain, A., Chaudhary, J., Gautam, M., Gaur, M., & Grover, S. (2024). Concept of mental health and mental well-being, its determinants, and coping strategies. *Indian Journal of Psychiatry*, 66(Suppl 2), S231–S244. https://doi.org/10.4103/indianjpsychiatry.india njpsychiatry_707_23

Pinto, P. (2023, July 24). *Impostor syndrome: The good, the bad, and the ugly*. LinkedIn. https://www.linkedin.com/pulse/impostor-syndrome-good-bad-ugly-pedro-pinto-mcc/

Reierson, K. (2023, June 17). *The importance of confidence in effective communication*. Illumination. https://medium.com/illumination/the-importance-of-confidence-in-effective-communication-a1fb66e2a5d5#:~:text=To%20communicate%2 0with%20confidence%2C%20you

The power of authenticity: Embracing your true self. (2023, June 1). Trust Mental Health. https://trustmentalhealth.com/blog/the-power-of-authenticity-embracing-your-true-self#:~:text=At%20the%20core%20of%20being

What is exposure therapy? (2022). APA. https://www.apa.org/ptsd-guideline/patients-and-families/exposure-therapy#:~:text=The%20exposure%20to%20the%20feared

Made in the USA
Coppell, TX
25 July 2024

35188921R00056